Space

whose humour and [illegible] helped us develop

Janet Nicholls
Helen Evans
Diana Hekt
Frank Hooper
Stuart McClure
Sali Mustafic

Introduction

The editing of most of these poems has been done by us all – me and the six poets here – in that intimate, critical, round-table setting in which so many poems make their first public outing; their first publication, in fact. And it's that passionate, committed response to poems in these early drafts, the excitement of seeing the better – or true – poem emerge, that has led to the publication of this pamphlet.

Here, then, you have four poems by six poets. Each selection shows the poet offering their own way of seeing and telling reflected in their individual styles. In playing some small part in collating these poems it struck me how the various stages poems go through are a part of a larger journey for both the poem and the poet. I hope, for each of these poets, that this publication signifies the next, important, step in that adventure.

Greta Stoddart
Devon 2011

Contents

Janet Nicholls

Janet's passion is to follow the seasonal round through the countryside, wherever she is; she sometimes writes about these places but more often just listens and watches.

Warblers

Little fidgets of spring;
thrill trillers,
happiness shouters.

Marmora's, Sardinian
and Cetti's warblers
agitate my footsteps
through mastic, Jupiter's beard
and wild olive scrub,
towards a winter dumped,
spring tossed beach.

But in the low tide silence
of bleached silver,
and the slow movement
of stone shadow,
she is not there.

The cleaner

I have cleaned my way through lives,
I have cleaned lives away.

I have dusted meaningless ornament,
the shoes of the dying,
the clocks that no longer chime,
the leaves that fall.

I have dusted chaos,
removing a fine surface of waste,
leaving no order behind.

I have polished silver lives of eating,
chased whirling gold.
I have sliced sunbeams with a broom,
swept sadness into tears.

I have cleaned my way through my life,
I have cleaned the life out of me.

Care

She heaves her bruised way on crutches,
an enchanted figure
in white DVT stockings and short white nightie.

'Janet must get out now.'
It's time to kick out my impatience
on golden chestnut and yellow lime leaves,
to have my head breezed by a rushing weir,
while seagull shadows fly across my face.

The river falls in a five-stepped wall of streams,
no chatter, no little complaints,
just two swans' necks
lining up with channels of white foam.

Otter

The Blackdowns pour brown,
pushing the Otter into red-drawing rush;
the smell of mud and ozone follows its course
as if gas were leaking along this valley.

Reeds shudder, bow over and lie with the pulling flow,
to spring up and start a different dance,
as flotsam is trapped and whirlpools shift
again and again
I walk the spate
towards freshwater bursting into the salt,
where it is pushed back by wave breaks of red brown scum
and pulled by the clatter and scrape of tide dragged stones.

I glimpse a woman in my backward glance;
she might have been you,
for this is your place too.
We would have sat side by side in front of the storm
and known each other's seeing,
as spray fingers its way up the runnels of red cliffs.

Helen Evans

Helen returned to poetry after a career in journalism. Last year she achieved a Master's Degree in Creative Writing with Distinction from the University of St Andrews. She seeks to sense the connections between faith, desire and creativity; and to explore the natural world in person and in poems.

Out of season

The saucepan dumped
in layby 94's
half-buried at an angle in the snow,
a shadow of dry grass
under its black plastic handle,
clear ice spilling over
its rim; the non-stick coat's
scoured off
in one great circle;
mountain hares have left
deep marks in the summer drifts.

I want to take a panful of their tracks
home in my warm car.

The jackdaw's

here on the tower floor with its wings spread
rigidly. The soft down has just begun
to dandelion away from its head
and charcoal neck, which is broken,
but its fledgling gape is still yellow inside,
bulging like a fungus.

It's landed in a scatter of dried
fragments of nest – torn paper, silver foil,
brittle twigs and wisps of fibreglass –
next to an age-blurred fallen gargoyle
and disinterred stone sarcophagus.

School-leaver

I spent that summer pigeonholing cheques
into alphanumerical order
behind the cramped machine-room's half-closed blinds,
fleeing at five to clock up thirty lengths,
each nine breast-strokes long, my goggled face
gulping in gobbets of air above water,
snorting out lustre-walled bubbles below,
again, and again, until I somehow stopped

pushing forwards – swam as though suspended
in the gap between one moment and the next,
hauling the pool's far blue edge towards me
with each heave of my arms, sensing the earth's
curvature scroll past on either side, then
watching myself from above, streamlined and flowing.

Engine test

silence
then the
intensifying whine of

turbine blades slicing through air
as the chalk subsoil judders under the peritrack
you look for the take-off and the sound shudders to a peak

but there's no movement on the runway and the noise
subsides, the ground settles, leaving rotating
blades winding down, revealing

goldfinches
brightly lit by
silence

Diana Hekt

Diana has lived in Devon for 25 years, the last 14 in Exeter, and written and performed poetry on and off along the way.

Love stone

You had been here for ages
I guessed, securely,

warm from the sun
to the touch of my soles

and how pleasant was that?
Perfectly flat.

As pure indulgence
I became one half enjoying

a relationship;
the stone itself the other.

Nightweighted

The sky struck *two*. Those clouds, cushioning
you, drifting through sleep,
were suddenly *alarmed.* Gone.

Awake on a bed of hard minutes
you try to rearrange the point of agony,
to spread it over all of you, thinly.

Time, however, has taken the other side;
you're up against yourself in slow motion,
control no longer yours to lose. You notice

the cover you would love, its patterns.
The workings of it have a history;
rules were obeyed. People had queued for hope.

You are amazed by the size
of each weightless second as it opens,
by its completeness in every detail;

while your body, wavy hot
or slab cold, stays out, low, laid down,
whether or not you choose to float

above the rumpled troubles of your bedscape.
So you ride the miles of another night
till five, when the painkillers will arrive.

The errand

The child, sent out with money
to fetch soap and butter,
returned with nothing
but a plum, and her first big lie.

It was dark in the shop, though
not yet dusk. Alone, the grocer
was staring at the ghost before him.
Please go away*!* he begged.

She stumbled and scrambled by boxes,
banged her funny-bone on an edge,
ran straight into all the fruit
in baskets outside the front door.

Her favourite – plums! She stole five,
savoured four on the way home.
She said she'd lost the money
and the grocer had given her a plum.

Meditation on noise and being

An hour to twilight
the man stood
at the reservation;
heavy traffic sped close by
his left shoulder.

Still as a skittle,
his back turned hard
against the constant approach,
he studied his car just ahead –
broken down in the fast lane.

Frank Hooper

I write plays and poems and am fascinated by language, especially the spoken language. For me the voice has to be developed so it can express all the nuances of sense, sound and feeling within a poem; and this finds its way into the writing.

Elegy

'The soul is a small portion of God' Diogenes

Little remains
when the house is gone

the half-hinged door
the neglected hearth

the staircase hanging
by a thread

only the wind and rain
through the broken window frame.

Little remains
when the soul is gone

only the traffic lights of the brain
and a half-remembered song.

Albertine

Endless fall of
pale, pink petals:

scent hangs heavy,
like bonfire smoke,
in the still air.
The ground cries for rain.

Time has ceased
for the small child
motionless
in the garden
with his mother calling.

Old now,
in a different garden
I stand still
smelling that rose.

Helen House

This is the house
that holds grief,
as wood anemones cradle
the new-born Spring.

This is the house,
where air is thin.

Within the house
there is a room,
within the room
a single bed,
on which the dead
child is laid.

A mother cradles her son,
just two-days old,
and sings him lullabies
and kisses his cold face.

Impotent hands clasp empty air;
the sea, moon-drawn, surges incessantly.
The cold stone sweats on the fetid shore.

*

The mooring ropes are slipped;
and the little boat follows the sun path

over the quiet sea
driven by the wind of heaven.

Corn ripens is gathered and ground, until
she finds a moored boat
on a slipway by the river's edge.

She does not know the way
but raises her sail
for an unknown land, where

marking her path
dark-blue violets glow.

The room

I remember that room.
The rasping,
gasping,
breath.

I remember the hallway
between the sitting room
and the kitchen.

How cold it was,
only the stairs
he could no longer climb,
and the letterbox
where the cold came in.

Confined in that room,
his bed there,
his chair,
where he lived
ate
and defecated.

The three steps across that cold barrier
he could not make,
it would take his breath.

Gradually, he ate less,
for swallowing,

for a moment,
obstructs the breath.

Gradually he spoke less.
He had to draw
breath after breath
rapidly,
so talked less and less.

His coffin stood
in that room.

Stuart McClure

My background is in Primary School teaching and Psychotherapy (Person Centred). I am a member of the Devon based group, Moor Poets; and have spent much of my life trying to escape everything by walking on Dartmoor and the South Devon coast path, though my greatest love is North Cornwall.

Hope Cove

Low tide, a fulcrum,
eagerness in the waves.

The furthest I've been out to sea,
past rocks where water is cradled

like dreams or memories.
I swam here once, held

by the density of salt
and belief in floating.

Now the north-easterly bites
through all my careful layers.

Boscastle

The sheer drop of it
down from the brow
to the gasp of the sea

that once bobbed
with sainted coracles
bringing the Irish version.

And before that, Phoenicians
sailing in like honey bees
for the blossoming of tin.

The cut of the valleys,
Valency and Jordan,
razoring to the flood plain,
braided in wedlock.

Out past the harbour wall
the gas and steam of the blow hole
hissing like a whale,
as the Atlantic fist strikes home.

Mayflies

Mayflies irritate the air
as they swarm from a hedge,

invoked by late April warmth.
They blunder in a brief frenzy,

oblige me to shut my mouth
to avoid the crunch
of small potent bodies.

Once, on the Moors, they were so thick
they formed an evanescent strata;
swirled when swatted like vapour.

I lean on a gate – a different climate –
the cool air finds me out.

This one lets in distance,
a far off estuary, pale with haze,

graduated light washing the hills.
For a moment
I am free, of the random fecundity,
the brittle cloud;

take back the grudge.

The clearing

The ringing of water;
a circle of burnt wood,
cracked-carbon.

Cut limbs of young trees
stacked in a square,
like a beginning.

On the upper path
among white stars of garlic
and the powder of bluebells,

the charred remains of a tree,
stump still rooted, figurative,
a fire sculpture.

I would wait for the sun
to fall on it –
a blessing or an omen –

but the ferry is crossing soon,
the boatman holds open the gate.

Sali Mustafic

I am a narrative life coach and former teacher whose fascination with language lies at the heart of all my writing. Inspired by the Romantics, Eastern European and post-modern poetry, I enjoy experimenting with form, style and content. While I like to use language to create new perspectives, I also strive to make poetry accessible and interesting.

As in the dark I listen

Tell me stories, sing me rhymes,
echoes in the darkness of long nights.

You sing of autumn moon
the mossy way through forest
and mountain wreathed in mist.
You sing of leaving me.

And you will leave and I will linger here
stars in my hair and flowers at my feet
incense drowsy in the darkling air.

Tell me stories, sing me rhymes,
Even in the dark of this long night.

Minutiae

The hands of the clock are stealing me
overtaking each other in haste over my life
my years are swallowed by seconds
don't blink – a stash of my life is lost in the blinking
I'm slipping – sand ash – through something I cannot reach

and somehow – in the falling – my mind's mirror is tumbled
I see the grains of me separate

each speck seeing its own-ness
clings – and we
                    fall slowly
taking the time
                    to breathe through seconds
and – breathing
                    settle
like snow

I see
the hand of the clock
the sixty seconds it takes
                              between
each demarcation
expanding the minute since the fall.

Dear Mum

You know how I always looked forward
as walking home I touched the hedge three times
with the fingers of my left hand
only the fingers – never the thumb
and allowed myself to step
on three cracks in the pavement
and how if I heard the ice cream jingle
I whispered three girls' names
before the music stopped

and you know how I always looked forward
to seeing your coat on the back of the kitchen chair
the one nearest the sink
hearing the radio – always a talk show at 4pm
and pouring tea from the pot
still hot on the table

You know I always looked forward
and yet
that day
it wasn't the hedge or the ice cream van
it wasn't the cracks in the pavement so
that day I must have looked back

and it must have been while I turned
that
you emptied and rinsed the teapot
turned off the radio

picked up your coat
and let yourself out
through the front door
as I came in at the back

I'm sorry Mum

If I do it again tomorrow
make no mistake ...

Snow

I am showing it all to you for the first time

The cold, the clean and the white
the purified world
I want you to hear its crisp
taste its newness
laugh in its exhilaration

A dog waits patient and ready

On the other side of the world in heat and under yellow sun
a man runs.

Where and when will you go?

Cover design by Tinker Mather

Tinker Mather worked as a painter before moving to writing and hasn't hesitated since, except to accept the kind offer of making the drawing for this pamphlet.

Janet Nicholls:	janarchernicholls@yahoo.co.uk
Helen Evans:	helennz@hotmail.co.uk
Diana Hekt:	hekt@blueyonder.co.uk
Frank Hooper:	f.hooper@tiscali.co.uk
Stuart McClure:	stuartmcclure@waitrose.com
Sali Mustafic:	sali@interbe.co.uk

Published by Hooper Publishing, July 2011

The Patch, Dolton, Winkleigh, Devon, EX19 8RJ
Tel: 01805 804432
Email: f.hooper@tiscali.co.uk

ISBN 978-0-9569744-0-2